Managing Your Image

in a week

LAUREL HERMAN

Hodder & Stoughton

A MEMBER OF THE HODDER HEADLINE GROUP

**the Institute
of Management**

The Institute of Management (IM) is the leading
organisation for professional management. Its purpose is
to promote the art and science of management in every
sector and at every level, through research, education,
training and development, and representation of
members' views on management issues.

This series is commissioned by IM Enterprises Limited,
a subsidiary of the Institute of Management, providing
commercial services.

**Management House,
Cottingham Road,
Corby,
Northants NN17 1TT
Tel: 01536 204222;
Fax: 01536 201651
Website: http://www.inst-mgt.org.uk**

Registered in England no 3834492
Registered office: 2 Savoy Court, Strand,
London WC2R 0EZ

Orders: please contact Bookpoint Ltd, 39 Milton Park, Abingdon, Oxon
OX14 4TD.
Telephone: (44) 01235 400414, Fax: (44) 01235 400454. Lines are open from
9.00–6.00, Monday to Saturday, with a 24 hour message answering service.
Email address: orders@bookpoint.co.uk

British Library Cataloguing in Publication Data
A catalogue record for this title is available from The British Library

ISBN 0 340 780 932

First published   2000
Impression number   10 9 8 7 6 5 4 3 2 1
Year   2005 2004 2003 2002 2001 2000

Cover photo from Telegraph Colour Library.
Typeset by Fakenham Photosetting Limited, Fakenham, Norfolk.
Printed in Great Britain for Hodder & Stoughton Education, a division of
Hodder Headline Plc, 338 Euston Road, London NW1 3BH by
Cox & Wyman Ltd, Reading, Berkshire.

■■■■■ C O N T E N T S ■■■■■■

I would like to dedicate this book to all my clients who have contributed to my experience and expertise over many years. It was their appreciation, support, increased confidence and achievements that helped me realise how important image really is!

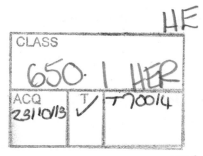

Your image is how the world sees you. This obviously matters most when people don't actually know you *as a person*. However, even if they do, they still have their own image of you. Sometimes, they tell us when we don't live up (or down!) to it.

In order to manage your image effectively, it has to be done in stages.

Sunday

You need to understand the importance of image to you and your career. We shall also explore the way that you can use your image to your own best advantage. Image is a composite – we will identify the various image ingredients that contribute to it.

Monday

Before we start the 'improvement, enhancement or development', you need to stop and think hard about what you would like your image to be. You then have to test how it actually is at present. This will help to determine your strengths and weaknesses and create a strategy for the rest of the week.

Tuesday to Friday

We shall be dealing with the image ingredients one by one in great detail. You will then be able to apply as much or as little practical advice as you think you need.

Saturday

By the end of the week, you should feel confident in the fact that you are now managing your image in a very positive way. As your confidence increases, and it undoubtedly will, your overall image will improve even more.

As life takes its normal course, it is sometimes easy to slip backwards. We shall therefore look at ways to help you maintain your achievement – and deal with sudden disasters!

By the end of this week, you can be confident of having a positive business image that will be viewed even more positively by others.

Understanding and using *your* image

Your image is others perception of *you*. In Britain we sometimes have a problem with the word image. We seem to believe that if one is only an image, our quality of person, let alone our ability and intelligence, are being disregarded.

Let us begin by being clear about our image. Whether you want it – or not; whether you like it – or not; whether you agree with it – or not; there is no doubt that to everyone besides family, friends and colleagues who actually know you as a *person*, you are *only* an image. However, the good news is that you are in control of your image. It stands to reason therefore that you should create, or adjust it and use it to the best advantage in both your personal and business life.

Overall, the right business image is one that says you are:

Adaptable	Creative	Organised	Sincere
Approachable	Experienced	Professional	Successful
Competent	Honest	Resourceful	Understanding
Confident	Intelligent	Sensible	On the leading edge

The Importance of *your* image as a tool of communication

The modern world is all about communication. It is essentially a visual one due to the universal influence of the screen, both large and small.

When an advertising agency or a film director wants to create a persona that you will 'read' instantly, they usually portray a stereotypical image that leaves you in no doubt. You can similarly choose to be a stereotype that is easily understood by others.

The first impression
Much has been written about the first impression and I do not think that anyone will deny its importance. We all admit to making instantaneous judgements about others; it is therefore obvious that others make them about us.

However, it is quite interesting to discover just how many *subconscious* assessments may be being made, either rightly or wrongly.

These will include a selection from:

Authority	Determination	Meticulousness
Ability	Dynamism	Orderliness
Age	Education	Personality
Aptitude: sporty, arty, etc.	Flair	Poise
Background	Geographical background	Political orientation
Career potential	Health & wellbeing	Race
Cleanliness	Honesty	Sense of humour
Confidence	Intelligence	Sincerity
Corporate commitment	Lifestyle	Social attitude
Creativity	Marital/family status	Social status
		Wealth

At least 30 different judgements about you – all in the first few minutes!

In business terms, if your image does not please the respondent – there is no way you are going to get a second chance. With luck, a substantial amount of conscious effort may begin to shift the judgement. However, often you will not get the opportunity or, even more importantly, you might not even realise that it is needed. Therefore, you must do your utmost to ensure that the initial impression you make is the right one (i.e. the one you want to give).

The corporate image
To a client, or indeed anyone, who only knows *you*, *you* are the organisation. Ensure that your image endorses how the-powers-that-be want the organisation to be seen – with a slight degree of individuality thrown in.

Empathy

An empathetic image can only be a distinct advantage when dealing with clients – or indeed within your own organisation. If you look like someone's 'kind of person' you will begin at a higher level of trust/confidence/ understanding and therefore communicate more easily and more positively.

A *typical* IT boffin would not appear to be terribly empathetic to a *typical* sporty, Health Club manager; a *typical* Creative Director in an ad agency would not seem to have a natural empathy with a *typical* traditional City Banker who may be an important client.

The importance of *your* image as a means to achievement

The look of success

Looking *successful* breeds further success. There is no doubt that if you look successful you will be viewed as successful. I am sure that you would prefer to do business with a person (or a company) with a proven track record which seems to be frequently chosen and approved by others. *Successful* implicitly implies that you are good at what you do.

Climbing the success ladder faster

Others with the same skills and ability as yourself but who already look the part may well receive the next opportunity or promotion. The advice often given is to look the part of the person immediately superior to you. If you do this, there will not even begin to be an issue about whether you look appropriate when the time comes for promotion. You obviously do. It will also help to get you noticed at the outset.

Some organisations send men or women who are being groomed for greater things, but whose image is not compatible with that required at higher levels, to an image consultancy. However, in other organisations, or in certain circumstances, the decision-makers may not bother, or have the inclination, to invest in their employees in this way.

Get it right *yourself* now and ensure that you are first in line for the next opportunity.

Increasing confidence
If every day could be a Look Good: Feel Good day, think how much less stressful and better our business lives would seem! I would be very surprised if you do not admit that you feel good when you know you look good. On those days, we often seem to get on swimmingly with others,

everything seems easier and accordingly we get better results. It is because when we have more confidence, our body language and our general aura are more comfortable which consequently brings out the best in others.

Easier communication also leads to a more confident and enhanced performance which will undoubtedly eventually increase chances of business success and promotion.

Being taken seriously
Irrespective of their image, (whether an impoverished artist or an eccentric professor) anyone who thinks, or appears, negatively – is rarely viewed positively by others.

When it comes to presence, pale grey is probably a graphic description of someone with almost zero presence. Someone who will not really be noticed or remembered. Remember, positive doesn't mean 'standing out' in a negative way, it means that you are noted and taken seriously for positive qualities, attitudes and ability.

You can measure presence as a percentage. To be seen as positive, you should aim for at least 75%.

Getting the best out of life
If you make the most of yourself as far as your appearance is concerned, more often than not you will get the best out of people and situations. We are not talking about personal beauty but a well groomed, well co-ordinated, 'successful' overall appearance which generates innate respect in others. This is no longer a premise but has been borne out by academic research. Even starting at the very beginning of life, pretty babies are talked to more by their mothers and by their siblings.

Besides image being important per se, the *right* business image can contribute a great deal to your career development.

The ingredients that craft *your* image

These are actually all the elements about *you* that together create the perception.

Your appearance
Wardrobe is very, very important but not to the exclusion of the other image ingredients. Everybody always centres immediately on clothes when thinking about image. A popular fantasy is that if you bought an Armani suit you would automatically look a million dollars. The sad truth is that you will not look any different than in your own two-year-old High Street suit – and you will be a lot poorer! The answer is in the way that you choose your suit, how you apply the finishing touch – fit, co-ordinate, accessorise appropriately – and then complete the picture through top-to-toe grooming. Then you can still buy in the High Street but look and feel a million dollars – having saved a small fortune!

It is also important that the feel and the cut of your clothes makes you feel good. If you are comfortable you are not constrained and that shows in your body language. Everything in your working wardrobe should always be flattering and appropriate to the situation in hand. For peace of mind, you should aim for *your* wardrobe to work for *you*. When your wardrobe works, your clothes answer all your needs and you will feel comfortable and complimented by everything within it. You therefore can get on with the important things in your life in the knowledge that what you are wearing and how you are wearing it, is right.

Your grooming overall should give an impression of cleanliness and impeccability, showing that you care about how you look i.e. attention to detail.

It includes nails and hands, hair, skin (make-up *for women)*, smell/hygiene, glasses/lenses, and teeth.

Your presentation
Your voice can dispel an image or, equally, can enhance it. We are not talking about accent. We are speaking about voice, pitch, speed, intonation, timing and contents. A high pitched squeaky voice indicates a nervous, flibberty gibbert kind of person. Not one you would possibly feel you would want to meet on many occasions, or have confidence in in business. A slow monotone with little change in pitch would seem to belong to a slow plodding person with little personality or 'oomph', let alone boring all listeners to tears!

Voice is therefore important in contributing to the actual image of the voice owner. However, a pleasant interesting voice is always a plus factor as people enjoy listening to it and therefore pay more attention.

Face and body language tells us a great deal about a person but often without us realising it at a conscious level. When we begin to look better – and therefore feel better – about ourselves, these messages often change positively as they are basically reflectors of our own confidence.

The need for manners and etiquette is said to be fast disappearing in the modern world. Personally, I believe that it is best to conform as it is still considered by many as most important. If you are not seen to practise this code, it could certainly count against you in certain situations. It is always best to know what is viewed as right and then at least you can make an *informed* decision about whether to use it or not.

Manners and etiquette are also a means of showing respect to others and that can certainly do no harm as long as it is not seen to be overdone, sycophantic or old fashioned.

Behaviour is somewhat different. It should be noted that your behaviour should always be congruent with the image you are choosing to portray.

Summary

Today, we have clarified:

- the reasons why it is so important to have the right image
- the components that make up the total image

Tomorrow we will test *your* present business image in order to plan what work needs to be done.

The importance of image

AS A COMMUNICATION TOOL

- It sends out messages about you.
- If the FIRST IMPRESSION isn't *right*, you don't get the chance to make a second.

- Empathy expedites business relationships.
- *You* are the corporate image – that is a position of responsibility in itself.

AS A MEANS TO ACHIEVEMENT

- A POSITIVE PRESENCE will be treated positively.
- Appearing 'successful' means, in crude terms, that people *buy* you. You must be good at what you do. Others will therefore want you too.
- Attractive people generally get the best out of people and situations.
- Looking the part of your superior may well aid climbing the ladder faster.
- The positive image cycle.

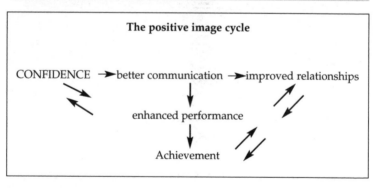

The positive image cycle

CONFIDENCE ➤ better communication ➤ improved relationships

enhanced performance

Achievement

The image ingredients

- APPEARANCE: Wardrobe and good grooming
- PRESENTATION: Voice, body language, manners, etiquette and behaviour

Laying the foundations

We have explored why this subject is so important to you
and your career and how messages about you are
transmitted by your overall image and by each image
ingredient. Now we must decide on our objective and
assess what and how much needs to be addressed.

Thinking about your present image

1. Watch TV and observe the commercials. The images
   being shown to you instantly create an impression in
   order for you identify the subject – and buy the product!

Identify images such as:

- Clean, houseproud suburban middle class man or
  woman
- Smart city banker
- Yuppie trader
- Successful sophisticated European
  business(wo)man
- Student at a red brick university
- Typical Oxford professor

By the same token we respond to stereotypes in real
life – and buy the product!
2. Can you picture the image of a successful ... (*whatever
   you do*)
3. When you see successful businesspeople, what tells you
   they are successful?
4. If appropriate, decide which adjectives describe your

organisation/company's corporate image. They should apply to you too.

5. Look at your superiors and decide if they look better presented than you – and in what way.
6. Are at least 75% of your working days Look Good: Feel Good days?

Thinking about your aspired image

You need to think hard about what the right image is for you, the necessity to achieve it and to commit to it. It needs to be an evolution, not a revolution. You will not – and should not change radically in a week. For this to really work, it must be a gradual development, a type of metamorphosis. As changes take place, you will feel good about yourself, especially if you are complimented by others. As you get used to the change and feel comfortable with it, you may well feel ready to take even more on board in a way that you were not at first.

We will be addressing different issues each day but you should continue to deal with these in weeks to come until you feel you have gone as far as you can with each one.

You need to test how you are seen by others to give you the framework to work with.

Your business image

1. Select the five adjectives that describe your present business image best.
2. Select the five adjectives that *you would like* to describe your business image.
3. Image is others' perception of you. It is also the way that you believe you portray yourself to others. It is useful to test how different these may be.

Ask the following to write down the five adjectives that best describe your business image:

- Three business colleagues/contacts who you do not know very well.
- Your superiors at work.
- Three others who only know you by telephone.
- Three people at work who know you well.

It would be sensible if possible to incorporate someone else's help who could organise this and then compile the list without you knowing who said what. This would remove any bias in the answers from people who do not wish to offend you.

Colleagues who don't know you very well			Those who know you only by phone			Colleagues who know you well			Your present image	Your desired image
1.	1.	1.	1.	1.	1.	1.	1.	1.	1.	1.
2.	2.	2.	2.	2.	2.	2.	2.	2.	2.	2.
3.	3.	3.	3.	3.	3.	3.	3.	3.	3.	3.
4.	4.	4.	4.	4.	4.	4.	4.	4.	4.	4.
5.	5.	5.	5.	5.	5.	5.	5.	5.	5.	5.

Compare the adjectives in each set with each other and then with the other groups.

Draw your own conclusions.

How others view your image ingredients
Ask family, colleagues and friends about your voice, your facial expressions, general demeanour, posture, walk, handshake, smile, your appearance i.e. grooming and clothes.

Remember some of this may be subjective and it should only be used as a guide.

Your presence

Think of people you know in shades of grey. Those with a 100% presence will be so grey they will be black! Those with a low rating will probably be hard to recall.

Ask three people who know you to assess you for presence on a zero to 100% rating or in terms of grey.

greyish white		pale grey		mid-grey		dark grey		almost black	
0	10	20	30	40	50	60	70	80	90	100%

Self assessment

By any relevant image ingredient, identify the reasons why you think you haven't worked on remedying this before i.e. your own obstacles.

Using a realistic and relevant standard, assess yourself regarding each image ingredient.

Wardrobe
Does your wardrobe work for you? Does it contain:

- Something appropriate for every normal occasion in your life e.g. conferences, meetings, weddings, funerals, dinners, etc. so that you don't need to rush out and panic buy
- Many combinations so that you are never bored
- Versatile garments that can be adapted from day to evening; work to leisure
- A capsule travelling wardrobe so that packing is a pleasure, not a chore

- Flattering, comfortable clothes that make you feel and look good
- Only clothes that you actually wear.

Voice

What does your voice imply about you, is it pleasant to listen to? Tape yourself and listen carefully. Can you be clearly understood? Think about whether people seem to understand easily what you are trying to tell them. Do they get impatient?

Non-verbal

What messages can you spot yourself that you may not have been aware of previously? Get out a few photographs and a recent video and write comments about yourself. Sit, stand and move in front of a mirror and really think about how you look, how you sit, how you gesticulate etc.

Grooming

Take a long hard and honest look at yourself.

Overall do you appear:

- Immaculate?
- Fit and healthy?
- Modern?
- Well groomed?

You have now given some thought to how you believe that you appear to others. You have also tested to what extent you were correct. Having worked out what you would like your image to be, you can use the information collected today. It should help greatly towards understanding what exactly you need to do to meet your goal.

Summary

- Think about your image – present and aspired
- Test opinion on your business image, your image ingredients, your presence
- Self-assessment: the obstacles that stopped you making change before now?
- Rate yourself on your wardrobe, your voice, your non-verbals, your grooming.

Voice and non-verbal language

Today, we are going to begin the necessary work on your image ingredients. We saw on Sunday that presentation is an integral part of your image. We shall now find out what you can do to improve your own presentation.

I was recently invited to talk to a very important group of men who I assumed would be cynical about the importance of image. I had to decide on a strategy that would make the necessary initial impact. Instead of arriving at the time stated, I waited to be announced and then *scurried* in. After being introduced by way of a big build up, I began in a high pitched, squeaky and breathless voice, allowing my words to trip over themselves. Meanwhile, I maintained a hunched shoulder posture and gesticulated wildly. After two or three sentences, I abruptly sat down to a horrified silence.

At this point my observers would have assumed me to be scatty, nervous, unconfident, untidy etc, certainly not management or leadership material! This judgement would have come primarily from my voice but my posture and body language would have further endorsed it.

Similarly, had I have sloped in and droned in a flat monotone whilst staring fixedly at my audience, they would have switched off pretty quickly. In this instance, they would have assessed me as someone slow, boring, uninspiring, lacking in personality, dull and ordinary; again certainly not of leadership calibre.

After a few seconds, I arose again, and standing quite upright with hands neatly by my side, I addressed the audience in my normal, hopefully pleasant and interesting, voice:

' Gentleman, *that* is the power of image!'

The voice

Academic research proves that 38% of the impression you make comes from the way that you sound and only 7% from what you actually say. In business terms, your voice should convey that you are:

- Informed
- Confident
- Responsible
- Authoritative
- In control
- Sensible
- Reliable
- Sincere

YOUR VOICE

should be	should not be
pleasant	rasping
interesting	squeaky
energised	booming
communicative	dull
convincing	monotonous
	mumbling
	flat
	high pitched

Be aware of the power of your voice and how you can use it to advantage.

Sincerity	Sound like *you* believe in what you say – or *they* won't believe in you
Tone	Select the appropriate one e.g. critical, angry, sympathetic
Inflexion	Use emphasis and 'throwaway' remarks
Clarity	Enunciate so that your words are heard clearly
Breathing	Listeners should not be aware of your breath – or lack of it
Pace	Don't leave them behind … or race ahead of yourself
Pause	Use frequently to aid absorption and comprehension
Pitch	Move up and down the octave for maximum impact
Passion	Sound like *you* care – if you want *them* to
Humour	Lightens the load but can subtly stress the message

Accents add variation and can induce interest, but do take note, if listeners often ask you to repeat yourself. This means that you are not easily understood – either by your clarity, your pace or your accent.

Think also about 'sounds' like grunts, clearing one's throat, a nervous cough, ums and ars, a lisp, grinding teeth etc. and what they convey.

Non-verbal behaviour

Non-verbal behaviour sends us messages – usually visual – that tell us a great deal about a person, almost always subconsciously. We make judgements often without even realising it. To ensure that you are being read as you would like, you need to check yourself out. The best way is to conduct research amongst friends and colleagues. Also ask people at work who hardly know you. In fact, they are the most valuable of all.

MESSAGES FROM NON-VERBAL BEHAVIOUR

- From our face: Eye contact

    Smile

    Facial expressions

- From our body: The way we walk, stand and sit

    Mannerisms and gestures

The way we look

Our face is probably the most telling as it is usually the point of focus. The expression 'eyes are the mirror of our soul,' says everything. *Normal* eye contact, as opposed to a false fixed stare, puts people at their ease – as does a warm, genuine and frequent smile. Our overall facial expression should be relaxed. It is the tensing of various muscles that demonstrate tension, anxiety, stress etc. Examples are winces, frowns, pursing lips, screwing up eyes, biting lips and a clenched jaw.

	Actual action	Message about you
Blinking rate	Accelerated blinking pattern	Nervous disposition
Eye contact	Fixed penetrating stare into recipient's eyes	I'm not letting you get away
		I am supercilious
	Avoiding eyes by looking everywhere else	I can't be trusted
Smile	The 'Salesman' – a fixed smile that does not come from the eyes	I don't mean a word of it
	A short smile delivered at the end of almost every sentence	I am very unsure of myself
Facial expressions	Puckered or pursed lips	I'm worried
	Twitches	I don't understand

	Actual action	Message about you
	Frown	I'm not confident
	Screwed up eyes	I'm stressed
	Tense lips set in tight line	I'm of a nervous disposition
	Frequent blinking Licking/Biting/Chewing lips	Scared/can't cope
	Clenching jaw	

Mr A (Anxious) came in to discuss how best he could provide his service to a major corporate. Throughout the meeting, although feeling quite confident, he wore a worried look, frowning often, as if this was his natural disposition.

Mr S (Salesman) came next, smiling a great deal but with a clenched jaw and eyes that were were narrowed and cold.

He was followed by Mr C (Confident) another competitor who appeared to be well at ease, smiling genuinely when necessary and ensuring normal eye contact with the interviewer.

Who would you be inclined to choose?

Mary noticed that people were always saying to her 'Cheer up love; it may never happen?' or asking her 'What's the matter?'

She finally twigged that she had a naturally unhappy expression.

She learnt to look happier, less pinched and smile more.

Result: Mary actually feels happier.

And more positive.

And receives better results.

In any selection process, such as a job interview, tendering for business etc. displaying anxiety or lack of confidence can never be in your favour. It will obviously make others believe that you yourself don't feel that you can deliver what is required.

The way we move

The authoritative person will make smoother open movements whilst the less confident one will make jerkier ones holding arms more tightly into the body.

Standing
We use posture like a mask – how much straighter and better we stand when we are dressed up or how we steel ourselves for something unpleasant by squaring our shoulders. We use it everyday without realising it and, by the same token, we read the signals in other peoples' posture without them having to utter a word.

When you are feeling tired, you slouch and droop. This also tends to happen when you don't feel confident and, if this is usual for you, the slouch can become your natural stance. Similarly, when you are angry you will lean slightly forward with your shoulders rising up towards your ears. If you tend often to feel angry or 'put out', this will certainly reflect in your posture.

Your positioning in relation to others should also be considered. Crowding in on someone's space can make them feel intimidated and overwhelmed. Standing too far apart, however, can be seen to convey aloofness.

Good Posture

- Stand with feet side by side
- Keep legs straight but not tense
- Breathe slowly and evenly
- Roll your shoulders back
- Lift chin slightly
- Imagine that puppet strings are holding up your head
- Your weight should be just forward of centre

Walking
Your walk illustrates how you command space – this reflects the extent to which one commands in other aspects of life too.

An assertive, purposeful person will take longer, slower and more definite strides. A meeker, less confident counterpart may scurry or, conversely, plod or shuffle.

Sitting
You should sit squarely and neatly, not slouch or sprawl,

within the chair. Your back should be firmly parallel to the back of the chair. Arms should be folded loosely on your lap – *not* folded tightly against your chest. *('I won't let you in'; 'I'm not open to ideas or approaches'; Don't mess with me').* Your legs should be folded or crossed tidily.

On one occasion I was invited to sit in on an assessment panel for appointing a Chief Exec in a local government position. I certainly won't forget the candidate who slouched to one side of his chair, leaning on his elbow which was splayed out on the arm of the chair throughout the interview. His whole manner displayed arrogance, even contempt, finally endorsed by him patronisingly complimenting the interviewer on her quality of question!

Mannerisms, gestures and actions

Not only do these again send subtle messages; they also can prove intensely irritating to others. The handshake is a very important action and a major contributor to the first impression.

	No	Yes
Handshake	The wet fish *A floppy soft hand gingerly offered*	A firm grasp with 3 or 4 regular up-and-down movements
	The pump *A resounding attempt to break your arm*	

The following show signs of dishonesty, anxiety or lack of confidence etc.:

- Fiddling with nails, objects etc.
- Flicking or touching hair
- Constantly touching, rubbing, pulling any facial feature
- Crossing and uncrossing legs
- Shifting from side to side
- Hand shielding front of face
- Rubbing hands together

The following show impatience, intolerance, boredom, lack of interest:

- Crossing and uncrossing legs
- Foot and finger tapping
- Folding and unfolding arms
- Head resting on hand
- Shrugs

Summary

Your presentation consists of 3 different elements.

- Your voice
- Your non-verbal language
- Your manners, etiquette and behavioue

Each one is important on their own merit but collectively they send out even more powerful messages about you

Before we consider your appearance, you need to work on your voice and your facial/body language. You should seriously take into account what you discovered from testing others' opinions and from your own observations.

If you feel that you really need more help, there are professionals who coach in these specialist areas.

Good grooming

We have looked at one aspect of your image, your presentation, now we shall look at your appearance. This consists of your grooming and your clothes.

How you look actually accounts for 55% of the impact in the first impression. It is therefore seriously important to do your best to get it right.

One of the main problems in the UK is the lack of importance attached to good grooming. It is generally believed – and propounded further by the media – that business image is basically about the clothes that you wear.

However, if the grooming and the finishing touches are right, they send positive messages. You can then often get away with a great deal less in the wardrobe department.

Good grooming	
Hair	Smell
Skin	Eyewear
Nails and hands	Teeth

Our basic British culture seems to have made it difficult for us to accept that how we look should be a priority. On the Continent, it is considered the normal way of life, just like enjoying *good* food and wine all the time, not just on high days and holidays.

Whatever the image, it should always be immaculate. In order to check yourself every day, a full length mirror is essential.

Hair ... on the head

Hair should always be clean, tidy, healthy and glossy. It is useful to get in the habit of always wiping down clothes – especially dark coloured ones – before leaving home in the morning to guard against 'snow' or errant hairs clinging to shoulders and collars and looking messy. Over-greasy hair should be washed daily but use a mild shampoo for frequent use and forget the old wives' tale that it will fall out! For flyaway hair, use conditioner and wash out well or use a leave-in one that is specially formulated.

Usual excuses/reasons for bad hair days

- It was the weather
- The humidity always does this
- I didn't have enough time this morning
- I'm overdue for a visit to the hairdresser
- My hair always needs 2 or 3 days to settle after it's been cut
- I'm growing my hair out
- It was a mistake by the hairdresser

There should never be any need for excuses to others or to yourself.

As far as business is concerned, there are two basic issues:

- Your hair needs to look very good *everyday*, not just occasionally
- Your hairstyle must be relevant to your life whilst also flattering and balanced to your face and your bodyshape.

The best advice is to try a new hairdresser. You may like the familiarity of someone you are used to but that probably is false economy. Try going up a notch, getting it cut really well and then see and feel the difference. A good cut is essential in creating a shape that looks good *everyday* with very little maintenance. Find a recommended hairdresser who, besides being skilled at their trade, will understand your lifestyle and its demands. Ask their professional advice on how to maintain your new style and the best products to use. A new hairdresser can look at you objectively as you are merely an image to him/her.

First ask them to describe what they would suggest doing *if* they had carte blanche.

A little word of warning: you may have a knee jerk reaction like ...

'I can't wear my hair in front of my ears' or *' I couldn't possibly have a side parting'*

Re-evaluate slowly, asking yourself 'why not?' Then find a suitable compromise together taking into account:

- Your normal regime. Whether you are office based, mobile, travel, entertain clients etc.
- Time *and your level of inclination* to look after your hair.
- Appropriateness to your job. Women: if you have long hair, it is not business-like to let it hang loose. Men: similarly, in traditional sectors, length should not hang over the collar.
- Your age. Women: I am often asked about the suitability of long hair over 40. I believe that most women approaching mid-life are more flattered by shorter hair diverting the eye up away from the areas that are naturally going down! Men: just be careful that you do not look like an ageing hippie!
- The proportion of the size of your head to your body. If you can, you should add or remove width or height to balance with the rest of the body. However sometimes there are other factors! Unfortunately, in the case of men or women who are very thin on top, there's really *nothing* that you can do with the size of your head, only your body!
- Your face and features. The face shape, angularity and fullness, the ears, nose, eyes, forehead etc.
- Hair type:
Texture – coarse, fine or normal
Inclination – curly, wavy or straight
Abundance – Thick, thin or normal

Receding hair for men
Unfortunately, there really is no miracle cure although several are advertised. My only advice is to accept what is happening in good spirit and concentrate on maximising all your other attributes. Do not be drawn to brush a few thin strands forward to try to disguise the thinning patch. Find consolation in the fact that many women find baldness extremely attractive – and toupées really naff.

Colour for women
I would like to suggest that once you have dealt with your make-up, you take a new look at your hair colour in relation to your *current* skin tone. Your hair should provide a definite and flattering contrast to your complexion.

As time passes, hair pigment fades – as does that of the skin. It can often add interest to add subtle lowlights or highlights. Strategically placed, they can also emphasise good features or divert from the negative ones. By adding a three-dimensional effect, they also make the hair look thicker as well as adding more body.

Hair ... on the face

Men
As this is a rather controversial issue, it would seem prudent not to provoke any prejudice and just be clean-shaven. Even so, it must be said that designer stubble and other facial hair may be highly acceptable – even desirable – in creative, IT and other contemporary sectors.

However, moustaches and beards are considered predominant features and the ones that you would be described or remembered by. If you have good features, why not let others focus on those instead?

There is no doubt that visible hair in the ears or nostrils is unsightly – and ageing.

If you are *blessed* with bushy eyebrows, they will grow bushier and closer together in time and overtake your face. Remember Dennis Healey? They can be easily pruned with the razor or tweezers.

Women
Check that no facial hair is visible. A visit to your local beautician can deal with it very effectively and painlessly and should be considered a top priority.

Teeth

Smile as often as genuinely possible to reveal good teeth. If they are not evenly coloured or whitish, visit the dentist and enjoy professional cleaning by the hygienist. If necessary, consider some cosmetic dentistry such as straightening, chemical whitening or veneers.

Eyewear

Unfortunately for us all, as they are costly to replace, glasses are now a fashion item that dates very quickly.

You need to make sure that:

- they suit you – experiment with all types of different styles using a friend or colleague as a sounding board.
- you're buying something that won't wear you – you want other people to notice you, not the glasses before you.
- they fit you. Usually, they should not be wider than your face, hide or contain your eyebrow. They should not rest on your cheeks. Constantly pushing them on your nose, often unconsciously, can be irritating.

If you wear lenses, check that you wear them unobtrusively; bulging eyes – or ever-blinking ones – are rather off-putting.

Glasses – the choices

Frames

- rims or rimless
- thick or thin rims
- large or small
- metal or other materials
- the colouring
- round or angular lines

Lenses

- tinted or opaque lenses
- shaded or uniform lenses
- plastic or glass lenses
- special light changing feature

Nails and hands

Hands should always look clean and well cared for. Hand creams are readily available that moisturise the hands and nourish the nails.

Nails should be clean, smooth and well shaped. Bitten nails are never acceptable. As well as looking unsightly, they demonstrate nervousness and inability to cope under pressure.

Cuticles should be neat and soft. If they appear scraggy or

over thick, push them down with an orange stick and apply a little cuticle cream nightly.

Nails should have some length, but not be like talons. They should be filed into an attractive rounded or square shape. Always use polish to some degree together with a base coat and a topcoat for a professional finish.

For women: Whether a soft pale pink, a French manicure or a muted tone, a varnished nail demonstrates both attention to detail, a feminising and personal touch to the work 'uniform'. Shocking pink, bright red etc. are inappropriate as are blue, mauve, sparkles etc.

Smell

We should always smell fresh and clean. As I often have to deal with these ever so sensitive problems in my day-to-day work, I would like to briefly bring them to your attention for you to consider whether any could apply to you.

An underarm deodorant is essential together with an eau de cologne/after-shave for men and perfume/eau de toilette for women. There is unlimited choice of scents which grows by the week. Choose something that is personally pleasing but pleasant and obvious to others whilst not overpowering.

If you tend to perspire, be very diligent about keeping clothes clean. *Odour* is caused when new perspiration meets stale perspiration.

Hair and skin should *smell* fresh and clean as well as appear so.

Feet can smell very cheesy. You can easily test by sniffing your shoes – and socks/stockings – when you take them off.

You can buy shoe, feet and hosiery deodorants and ensure that you air your shoes, never wearing them two days running.

Clothes – both under and outer – absorb body, cooking and smoking odours. Underwear and shirts must be washed daily and other garments should be left to air freely once removed. Although everything that you wear must always look pristine and smell fresh, be aware that frequent washing and dry cleaning do take their toll.

Keep a toothbrush and mouthwash at work to refresh breath at lunchtime and after work if necessary.

These are things that most of us take for granted. If everyone knew and practised them, there would not be any need to comment on them. But there is.

Case study

Recently I was asked to deal with a senior Bank Manager who didn't smell as he should – particularly on a hot summer's day. It was so bad that his secretary had left and the current one was thinking of following the same course. Hints had been made but fallen on deaf ears. Had it remained unchecked it would have had a detrimental effect on the man's career and limit his professional prospects.

However a little *direct* word in his ear resulted in a happy ending.

Skincare for men

Today the men's cosmetic market grows day by day as more and more men realise the importance of looking after their skin. Skin should always look good – unblemished, clean with an even and healthy colour. As dead cells can make the skin's surface uneven, exfoliating once or twice a week keeps it looking alive. Excessively greasy skin can be helped by the regular use of facemasks and tonic to cleanse and close pores whilst extra dry skin can benefit from a richer moisturiser. Facials are a pleasant and relaxing treat but also help to keep skin deep cleansed and moisturised. There are several product ranges which are especially formulated for men such as Clinique, Body Shop or Boots and several of the Clarins products are very suitable. Good shaving is essential to the appearance of your skin.

Before shaving:

- Wait at least half an hour after you get up in the morning to allow facial muscles to tighten and give whiskers a chance to stand away from the skin.
- Wash first with warm water to remove dirt and grime and soften bristles. This also improves razor glide as the texture of beard hair is like that of copper wire.
- Massage in your chosen shaving cream to lubricate skin and soften beard.

Shaving:

- Always soften with warm water before shaving. It is often a good idea to shave in the shower.
- Shave jawline and cheeks first, then neck, upper and lower lips and lastly the chin, where the whiskers are the thickest.
- Shave in the direction of the natural beard growth – do not go against the grain!
- Rinse your razor often to prevent clogging. Shaving can remove three skin layers, so do not shave over the same spot several times.
- Wet shaving is kinder to the skin, though on a regular basis it may be irritating to men with dry or sensitive skin who should consider alternating electric and wet shaving.
- Prepare the bristles for a more comfortable electric shave with a pre-electric shave product which improves the movement of the shaver to help prevent razor burn.

After shaving:

- Splash your face with warm water. Gently pat dry with a soft, clean towel
- Soothe and lightly moisturise skin. If you feel moisturiser leaves your skin too oily, apply an oil free gel which does not leave a greasy after-feel and is also mildly medicated.

Skincare for women

You do not need to spend a fortune or have a cupboard full of products to have a healthy and blemish free skin.

Daily essentials

- Cleanse scrupulously with milk, cream or lotion.
- Use a tonic if you have a particularly greasy skin.
- Nourish nightly to replace what is lost through ageing and the environment.
- Moisturise appropriately for your skin type – well-chosen moisturisers will never feel greasy and should be easily absorbed.

An extra note for those who are getting 'older'. Stop worrying ...

'Wrinkles are just a test of time ... they don't touch the soul' *anon*

Pass the test with distinction – and ignore them. Look well groomed and sophisticated; create a positive image and no one will even notice them.

Weekly extras

- Exfoliate, even lips, once or twice to keep skin looking alive.
- A facemask will deep-cleanse, moisturise and make skin look and feel fresher.
- Eyebrows should be plucked to keep them tidy.

(Survival kit and pick-me-ups: See Saturday)

Make-up

This is one of those very controversial issues that comes up time and time again.

Women in business should wear make-up *that is visible* as part of the groomed finished look. Visible does not mean thick, mask-like or plastered on. It means flattering as it is used to even and enhance skin tone and facial features.

The reasons for wearing visible make-up

- A survey carried out in the US proved that women who wear make-up earn 25% more than their counterparts who don't.
- The invisible (natural) look is not appropriate for the professional woman who needs *to show* that she is well groomed.
- With the level of pollution and the danger from

harmful UVA and UVB rays today, make-up should be considered a protection.
- Very few women are at their most attractive in their natural state, particularly as the years creep on. It can only make sense to use *and appreciate* the help that is available over the counter.

The reasons why you may say you don't want to wear visible make-up

- **I feel uncomfortable and dirty.**
  If you are unused to something, you would undoubtedly feel different, and probably uncomfortable, to begin with. If you were told that you had to wear glasses, you would feel very peculiar the first week, a little less the week after and, within a month, you would feel like you had always been wearing them. It is the same with make-up.
- **I don't want people to notice me.**
  Anything that is different is often treated with suspicion, and sometimes fear, and commented on negatively. I would start first with a little mascara and a new eyebrow shape: then wear a more defined lipstick shade. After a little time, wear visible foundation with some subtle blusher. Gradually you will achieve the objective without hearing comments that may undermine your confidence.
- **It will cost too much.**
  The High Street ranges are very reasonable and, as

you grow more confident, you can begin to
experiment and invest a little more.

- **It takes too long in the morning.**
  When you don't know what you are doing,
  everything takes longer. Once shown the way, your
  daily make-up regime certainly should take no more
  than five minutes and everyone can spare that. It is
  just a matter of committing to making this a priority
  like brushing one's teeth or bathing.
- **It's too difficult and will take too much effort.**
  It will not be once you know *how* and *what* to do.
  Don't you feel the same with anything that is new –
  each new computer programme, a new car etc?
- **I just don't know what to do.**
  Well, you will by the end of today!
- **It's just not me.**
  Of course it's not – if you're not used to it. But *you*
  are what *you* want *you* to be. Find a look that is
  comfortable for you.

Your basic daily make-up

Skin

- **Colour correctors**. If your skin tone is very uneven,
  very pale, sallow, blotchy, or with very high colour it
  will benefit from a colour corrector applied very
  sparingly in the relevant areas.
- **Concealer**. Where there are spots, age spots, scars
  or lines that still show, work in concealer very
  sparingly from a dab on your hand with a lip or
  special concealer brush.

- **Foundation**. This should even out texture and colour but not mask or hide your skin. Most of us are best with the water-based foundations that offer medium coverage. Your foundation should be your main investment so buy carefully by testing colour at jawline or on the neck. Apply small dots of foundation over your face with a cosmetic wedge, a Ramer baby sponge or a special brush.
Blend all over the face with downward and outward strokes and ensure it is taken out to the hairline, under the chin and fade into the neck colour. If you have used corrector or concealer, blend in at edges but do not cover totally with foundation.
Look straight ahead into a mirror facing daylight (or lit from the top at night). If you can see shadows and blemishes, you need to add a lighter shade foundation and gently apply it with your little finger, or a brush, on all those areas.
- **Powder**. Dip a felt powder puff in translucent loose powder and then *firmly* press into your skin, including eyelids and mouth. If you prefer a more natural look, or if you have very dry skin, just powder the nose, chin and forehead to reduce the shine. Brush off excess with large clean brush or cotton wool dipped in cold water and squeezed out well. Compressed powder should only be used for topping up during the day.
- **Blusher**. Choose tawny shade to define cheekbones and a second blush colour (amber, coral pink or dusky) to give you some natural looking colour.

Shading: Suck in cheekbones and apply shading slightly in triangle under cheekbones. Blend in very well with clean brush or powder puff.

Blush colour: With an upward and outward motion move the brush up the apple of the cheeks to the temple to give a healthy glow and repeat until the necessary depth of colour is reached.

Eyes

- **Eyebrows**. If your eyebrows are not a neat shape, pluck them or have it done first professionally as a guide. A good eyebrow shape frames your eye and opens it up, making it look larger and more awake. Brush eyebrows to remove excess powder and then lightly pencil in a flattering frame for your eye. Choose a colour close to your natural eyebrow unless you are very fair.

- **Eyeshadow**. Load your eyeshadow brush with a lightish natural powder eyeshadow (natural looking beiges or soft greys are safest) and cover eyelid area.

  Load a sponge applicator (for densest colour) or an eyeshadow shading brush (for more subtle application) with a darker shade (brown, grey or navy). Find the socket line; sweep this on and above this line to create an arc. Blend well with a clean brush.

- **Eyeliner**. Use a pencil or eyeshadow on a very fine brush to line your upper and lower eyelids – dry for softness, wet for stronger definition. Dot initially and then smudge together.

Only take the line three quarters of the way towards inner corners if your eyes are set close together.
- **Mascara.** Optional: Use eyelash curlers *first*. Apply one or two coats of mascara allowing each to dry thoroughly before applying the next. Comb lashes to separate with a special lash comb.

Lips

Using a tissue, blot lips to remove any excess grease. With a sharpened lip pencil, or lip brush loaded with slightly darker colour lipstick, draw a neat line around the edge of lips using short strokes. You can adjust your own lipline slightly if necessary.

Powder to set the line and fill in with your chosen shade, blending it with the line. Using your tissue, blot and apply a second coat. Always touch up your make-up at lunchtime and refresh in the evening.

Forget the obstacles and commit to making this a priority. I assure you that the compliments that you will receive and your increased confidence will make it all worthwhile. You need to achieve a daily make-up regime that is quick, appropriate to your life, easy to apply, up to date, and one that makes you feel at your best every day.

Make-up tips

- Buy very good brushes that you can control.
- Clean your brushes in soapy water once a week and let them dry naturally.
- Don't hoard foundation; when it separates it has turned rancid. Bin it.

- Use a lipbrush to use up lipstick to the very bottom.
- Use a cleaned mascara wand from a finished mascara to brush eyebrows and separate lashes.
- If you bought transparent mascara – a useless buy – it can be used as a finishing gel for eyebrows.
- The best time to apply moisturiser is before a bath to allow it to penetrate your skin.
- When buying foundation:
  - Go with naked skin.
  - Select 2 or 3 shades nearest to your jaw and neck colour.
  - Always check in daylight.
  - Buy a shade lighter also for shading and a concealer to match.
- You can apply dark brown or grey eyeshadow with a fine brush for a very natural looking eyebrow.
- Blend a tiny dot of concealer on the outside corner of your eye where the top and bottom lashes meet and see how wide-awake you look.
- In hot weather store pencils in fridge before sharpening to prevent them breaking.
- For a more natural look, wipe the mascara wand with a tissue to remove excess.
- For lip colour that fades, try a fixative or fill in lips entirely with pencil then applying lipstick. Blot and powder lightly. Repeat two or three times.
- For compressed powders e.g. blusher or eyeshadow, load brush first i.e. sweep the brush over palette and tap several times to remove excess colour.

Survival kit

- Esteé Lauder crème concealer in barely mauve is a great base and will prevent your eyeshadow from streaking. It is also good for correcting dark shadows under eyes and around the inner corners of the eyes.
- Touche Éclat by YSL – marvellous for tired shadows under eyes and lines.
- Flash Balm by Clarins wakes up tired looking skin.
- Issima Midnight Secret by Guerlain makes you look like you have had a good night's sleep – even with a heavy hangover.
- Dr Nelson eye mask.
- Elizabeth Arden 8-Hour Cream – great for dry skin. Can also be used as a conditioning lip-gloss.

Fixing make-up mistakes

- Use a little moisturiser to thin out too heavy foundation or to deal with cakey concealer.
- Use loose powder to reduce too much blusher, too dark eyeshadow or too hard looking eyeliner.
- Use a cotton bud with a small amount of eye make up remover – non-oily – and remove smudge. Re-apply foundation and powder to re set.
- Clean up a smudged lip line with a cotton bud dipped in make-up remover. Re-apply foundation then re-define lip border and powder.

We have now addressed all the aspects of grooming to give you an immaculate, fit and energised business image. Grooming is very important but you have to get the clothes right as well. Tomorrow we will consider generally what clothes are considered *right* for business and on Friday we will apply the information to your own wardrobe.

Summary

Good grooming is about your:

- Hair
- Teeth
- Nails and hands
- Eyewear if relevant
- Smell
- Skincare:
  - Shaving for men
  - Make-up for women

The business wardrobe

We have now sorted out all aspects of your grooming. Your hair, skin, nails, hand, teeth: all aspects of *look* are absolutely spot-on. Your skin, hair, body and breath should *smell* just as good.

Now we can get on to the upholstering – the clothes. However this is a really big subject. Today, we are going to consider what business wear consists of in general terms and then help you identify what it means for you.

A positive business image is conveyed by your clothes always being immaculate, contemporary, stylish and appropriate.

Positive business image	
Competent	Organised
Professional	Attention to detail
On the leading edge	Successful
Open, friendly, approachable	Sensible

Clothes should be immaculate – meaning well pressed, tidy, spotless, hemlines even, no threads hanging and buttons secured. There should be no dandruff or stray hairs on collar or shoulders.

Contemporary clothes are advisable rather than old fashioned but that certainly doesn't have to mean up-to-the-minute. To be stylish is to be aware of fashion while not being controlled by it. Fashion is what we're given, style is what we choose; fashion is today whereas style is perennial. Style is about confidence; not about cash.

Clothes should be appropriate to:

- **the sector**. Some sectors, like the City, education, the creative and voluntary sectors that most definitely have a certain image. Whatever the sector – and you might be involved with several – you are still relaying positive messages about yourself and your job through your overall image.
- **the location**. The demands – and variations – of a cosmopolitan metropolis, or of a smaller provincial city, are certainly very different from those of a small industrial town or, indeed, a rural market one.
- **the weather and season**. It is not just the practical aspect but certain fabrics look inappropriate at certain times of the year. It is more than just the colour, it is also the texture.

- **the corporate image**. If your company does have an image, make sure that you reflect it whilst also portraying your own individuality.
- **your status**. Check that you look the level that you are – or higher.
- **your aspirations**. It is said that if you look the part of the next rung on the ladder, you are most likely to be chosen for the role.
- **the personal factors**. Your age, your bodyshape, your personality, your lifestyle and your budget.

Although it would be nice to spend a great deal of money on our wardrobe, that is really not the basis of a positive and successful business image.

Belief

If you spend a fortune on your clothes, you would look like a million dollars

Truth

You may *feel* like a million dollars but it really ends there. You actually would *look* no different than you do in your normal High Street togs ... and you would be a great deal poorer!

The answer

How to look a million dollars without actually spending it:

- Choose investment garments *with skill*
- Ensure they fit and flatter

- Co-ordinate and accessorise correctly
- Compliment and complement with good grooming

Let us first define what is generally accepted as business dress for the life you lead.

Business wear for men – the suit

- Look around shops and department stores that specialise in business clothes
- Observe appropriate professional/business men on TV and cinema
- Look at pictures on the business pages to gauge what is generally acceptable

TIP

Many men find their trousers go very shiny. It is useful to buy two pairs of matching trousers and rotate them. In any event, you really shouldn't wear the same suit two days running.

Fabric

The suit should always be of a medium weight fabric (350–400 gms) so that it hangs well. Cool wool is always the best alternative, possibly supplemented by a small proportion of man-made fibre to make it more crease-resistant and hardwearing. It is always advisable to avoid synthetic fibres if you perspire.

For warmer weather, the fabrics can be lighter weight (250–300 gms) but don't buy cotton or linen suits unless you want to look like a ragbag. It is only those suave Italian fashion models who seem to get away with making creases look desirable!

Colour

Always choose a darkish suit but that doesn't mean limit yourself to a wardrobe of plain grey and navy. When the time comes for shopping, look around as there are many acceptable variations. There are low-key checks or stripes that add interest, many degrees of greys, blues and brown hues – even very subtle greens. Do try black – but trust your eye. If you think you look like an undertaker or a headwaiter, leave well alone! However, black with a stripe, check or texture may well be the compromise and an interesting addition to the closet.

Subtlety and sobriety

in colour, shape or texture

does not *have to* mean

dull or boring

The only time to wear a lighter coloured suit is in spring, summer, or very early autumn when a paler grey, a French (lighter) navy, taupe, camel or Houndstooth check can look very good. But do remember the limited practicalities – and always finish your outfit with the right shoes.

Style
As it takes some time before styles radically change, there are certain elements that will help you check that you do not look really out-of-date:

- Lapel width
- Jacket length
- Buttoning style
- Trouser width
- Pocket style
- Back vents

Smart/casual

In certain areas there is a current trend towards a *dress down* policy and a more Euro-look based on co-ordinates rather than on the business suit. If you have noticed the acceptability of this within your own business life, or if you often travel abroad on business, consider a jacket or two to wear with co-ordinating trousers.

Choosing the jacket
The choices are:

> • **A blazer** – This can be single/double breasted and always tailored.
> • **'Sports jacket'** – This can be either single/double breasted and tailored, or more unstructured for even less formality.

Classic colours are navy and black but contrasting shades like bottle or olive green, antique gold, burgundy, camel, toffee etc. are a little more interesting whilst still perfectly acceptable. If appropriate to your personality, job and status, aqua, mid blue and rust are rather more adventurous. All will look fine but again *only* if twinned with dark trousers for the most formality; and chinos, cords or tailored jeans for least.

You could now be a little more daring with tweeds, mixtures, and checks as long as they do not appear too loud and overall are of subtle colouring.

This dress code has given rise to a great deal of angst among us Brits to whom the words *smart casual* are often a total enigma. However it really is very easy once you know how. There is a very wide range of *how* smart and *how* casual starting with a smart tailored jacket coupled with dark trousers, which is really only one degree less formal than the suit.

Choosing the trousers

The trousers should be tailored, similar to suit trousers, of wool or wool mixture and in a dark colour for the maximum business-like look. Cords and chinos – tailored like trousers and not like jeans – add further informality whilst denim/moleskin etc. jean styles go even further towards a casual image.

Lighter shades and weights only become appropriate in warmer weather and should always look compatible with the jacket, e.g. winter 'brushed' cotton looks fine with winter tweed but summer weight or colour cotton would not.

Level of smart/casual formality

Worn with tailored dark trousers ...

Most formal

A blazer with a white/cream/pastel shirt and tie

A sports jacket with a white/cream/pastel shirt and tie

A blazer or sports jacket with a co-ordinating casual shirt and no tie*

A blazer or sports jacket with a crew or polo neck*

A blazer or sports jacket with a t-shirt*

A leather or suede jacket or other blouson with a co-ordinating casual shirt and no tie*

A leather or suede jacket or other blouson with a crew or polo neck*

A leather or suede jacket or other blouson wtih a t-shirt*

Least formal

*Even more informal but worn with tailored cords, chinos or smart jeans.

An option for those who feel comfortable wearing it is to match an appropriate suit – usually of a fashionable variety – with a black or white crew neck, t-shirt or sweater.

Update 2000
Jackets are:

- Mostly single breasted with three buttons.
- Double breasted is still popular for the broad shouldered or those who are a tad portly.
- The jacket should finish at the point where your thumb ends when you have your arms hanging straight by your sides.
- The bottom button should always be left undone.
- Pockets are mainly inset – not flaps.
- Most jackets have a single or double vent.

Trousers are:

- Straight, roughly 8 inches wide at the hem and without turn-ups.
- Mostly unpleated at the waist but a single pleat or double is very much more flattering – and comfortable – for the not so slim.

Business wear for women

Your clothes should always be chosen in a medium weight fabric so that they hang well.

It is best to always go for darkish shades but don't limit yourself to a wardrobe of plain grey and navy. When the time comes for shopping, look around as there are many acceptable variations on standard colours. Try rose, burgundy, olive, khaki, bottle, French navy, air force blue, teal, charcoal, taupe, terracotta, cinnamon, toffee, etc. Also consider low-key checks, stripes, tweeds and woven textures that add further interest. Avoid details like novelty buttons, appliqués, fringing at all costs, both in terms of appropriateness and of shelf life. For the sake of propriety, business wear should always include a jacket.

Jackets
The suit or jacket should be simply elegant, tailored and not quirky or extreme. Never be too sexy – i.e. tight, short or revealing – that does not mean *not* fitted or *not* shapely. In terms of formality, the order could be considered:

Most formal   1. A skirt suit* or a jacket with matching dress
              2. A trouser suit.* There is a fierce debate over the appropriateness of the trouser suit
              3. A dress with a co-ordinated jacket
              4. A knitted 2 or 3 piece
Least formal 5. Jacket and co-ordinating skirt or trousers*

*This is dressed up or down by the use of accessories and tops.

Skirts

Straight skirts are the most elegant for all shapes and sizes – providing they fit well. Even if your hips are rather bigger than the rest of you, a straight skirt is the only universally flattering modern shape.

Length should currently be somewhere from just above the knee to just almost covering it. If you really will only wear a long skirt, it should be very long but still showing some leg above the ankle.

Trousers

For business purposes, wear only tailored trousers in a cool wool type fabric/mixture with a narrow to medium wide straight leg ... and definitely not leggings, cut-offs, drainpipes, Capri pants or jeans.

Tops

Keep tops simple too – and not too skimpy! V or round necks sit best under most jackets as they create a flattering frame to the face. Lowish necks are not suitable for office wear as they may send out the wrong messages and distract. In any case, when worn under a jacket they are usually not as flattering to either the jacket or the wearer. To adapt to smart casual, you can include smarter knitwear worn instead of a jacket and sweaters instead of blouses or tops.

Now that we have defined what is generally appropriate for both men and women, you must sort out in your own mind what is right for you and your job. Tomorrow, we must ensure that you have *your* wardrobe that works for work.

Summary

Business wear must always be:

- Immaculate
- Contemporary
- Stylish
- Appropriate to:
  the sector
  location
  weather
  the corporate image
  your status
  your personal factors – bodyshape, personality, etc.
  your aspirations

Whatever the garments chosen, whether a suit or co-ordinated separates, it is imperative that the finishing touches are applied correctly.

- Good grooming
- Appropriate accessorising
- Clever co-ordinating
- Flattering fit

They will make all the difference.

Your wardrobe that works for work

Everyone needs *their* wardrobe to work. They can then get on with the important things in life in the knowledge that they always know *what* to wear and *how* to wear it. For working men and women this is even more imperative.

Now that we have established what is appropriate for your business image, you need to check out your own wardrobe and then decide what needs to be adjusted or added.

The *work wardrobe that works* should contain:

- An easily extracted capsule wardrobe to ensure that packing is no longer a chore.
- 100% items that you wear – no more mistakes.
- Something for every occasion – no need to panic buy.
- Items that reflect your selected self-image.
- Comfortable, practical and flattering garments that are 100% right for you.
- Less which is more – proper planning creates more permutations.
- Clothes that earn their keep – crossover from day to evening; work to play.

The *work wardrobe that works* is not a general formula; it is a personal philosophy based on:

- **You** – *Your* lifestyle, image, personality, bodyshape and budget
- **Wardrobe management** – Edit; Audit; Plan
- **The finishing touch** – Appropriate accessorising, clever co-ordinating, flattering fit and good grooming
- **Intelligent shopping** – Saving time, cost and effort whilst eliminating mistakes

You

- **Your bodyshape** – the shape and proportion are more important than the actual size
- **Your seasonal budget** – be realistic – you will need to regularly add to your wardrobe for it to work
- **Your personality** – you must wear the clothes, they must not wear you
- **Your chosen image** – that is already established: a successful business (wo)man
- **Your lifestyle** – give a rough assessment of the percentage of your time spent on each activity and the number of different outfits that you need for each.
  SC = Smart/Casual
   S = Smart

% time spent	Activity	No of outfits needed	Classification SC/S
	Work (conferences etc)		
	Work (normal)		
	Work related (social)		
	Private (social)		
	Sport		
	Interests, leisure		
	Holidays		
	Children (School transport, activities)		
	Other: e.g. Voluntary work etc.		

Wardrobe management – Edit

We must now examine and sort your present working wardrobe.

(*applies to women only)

- Remove everything that is not the current season.
- Put exclusively eveningwear at one end and the really casual at the other.
- You should only be left with your mainstream daywear.
- Separate all your suits, trouser suits, dress and jackets etc. into individual items*
- Hang everything on uniform hangers in sections – i.e. suits (only men), skirts,* dresses,* jackets, trousers and shirts/blouses*/tops* so that you can now see clearly what you have.

You now have to be very honest with yourself.

- Set aside items that need attention – if you have not dealt with them within two weeks, eliminate them, as you probably never will.
- The time has come to jettison *anything* that you know is:
  - inappropriate
  - dated
  - shabby
  - not flattering
  - not comfortable
  - doesn't fit – and is unlikely to in the near future.

In other words, anything that does not feel and look 100% and you probably don't wear anyway.

Don't worry if the wardrobe is considerably reduced. You still will be wearing the same clothes. You just will be able to see them clearly, work out more combinations and plan what is needed to extend their use. Once you have de-toxed the main wardrobe, do the same with all of your accessories.

Most of us tend to want to keep our clothes for posterity. The trouble is that your shape, and the fashion shape, changes over time. Even if it doesn't appear old fashioned, what may have fitted – and flattered – few years ago certainly doesn't now.

Wardrobe management – Audit

(*applies to women only)

- List what you have left in categories:

Suits (men)	Skirts*
Jackets	Dresses*
Shirts (tops etc.*)	Coats and outdoor jackets
Trousers	Sweaters

- Create and list each outfit on a table with complementary accessories and classify them as SC or S

Men

Jacket	Trousers	Shirt	Belt	Shoes	Other	Sweater	SC/S

Women

Top layer	Bottom layer	3rd layer	Bag	Shoes	Other accessory	Day/ Evening	SC/S

If you haven't got the *right* pieces to complete an outfit, it can't be considered as an outfit. You must then judge whether the outfit itself warrants the completion. If it would, ensure that the new addition can also be used to create further combinations.

Wardrobe management – Plan

Check if your number of outfits answers your needs. Write a plan of what you *need* – and then what you *would like* to buy.

Don't be too specific

WRONG

I need another lemon shirt/top* to go with my grey suit because my old lemon shirt/top* is shabby

RIGHT

I need a new shirt to go with my grey suit so I will buy one that complements the suit that looks good and feels good on me that is appropriate.

Checklist

- A raincoat, coat or outdoor jacket? It should be large enough to sit well over your jackets.
- More suits.
- A jacket or blazer – if you have one, possibly add the other.

- Trousers: Should they be tailored or casual? Have you the all the basic colours – black, grey, navy and dark brown? What colours or fabric – what already in the wardrobe are you going to wear with them with?
- Shirts (tops*) to increase or update existing outfits *providing they are worth spending further money on.*
- Knitwear – to adapt smart to smart casual.
  Polo's and crews in basic colours like cream, black and navy are evergreens.
  For men: Ties are your individuality label. Would a new one *really* breathe new life into an old suit?
  For women: Perhaps a dress in a core colour would be useful to be dressed up or down – as needs be.

The finishing touch – appropriate accessorising

The etceteras
Umbrellas, glasses, your pen, wallet, folder etc. may all be noticed by others – be sure they are worthy of you.

For men

Shirts
Always wear cotton or cotton with a small amount of polyester with ties. Always check that the collar is ironed well and not showing any fray at the points. For choice, you can't beat white and cream but very pale grey, lemon, pale blue, mid-blue and pink are all generally acceptable. I

would recommend you to steer clear of the fashion items like checks, black, dark grey and all the deep shades unless fashion plays a big part in your life – and your career.

Cut away collars are the most popular, button-downs are usually considered more casual and tab collars hold the tie very tight giving a sharp point and a very Continental look.

Cuffs can be single or double and should extend beyond the jacket sleeve for smartness – about one quarter to one half an inch depending on your shape and height.

Short sleeved shirts never look elegant – under any circumstances.

For shirts to wear without ties, you can choose a much greater variety of colours, textures and fabrics. In fact, one could almost say that the heavier the appearance of the fabric, the more casual you would look. Wearing your normal suit shirt without a tie will never look *very* casual but, if you do, remember to always leave the top button undone.

Ties

Don't make your tie – or yourself – a joke with cartoon characters etc. Why would any man think his tie should be 'a bit of a laugh'. *Subtle* is the word I would go for – don't let your tie be the one thing that is remembered about you. The best ties are ones that co-ordinate to your suits and possibly include some small amount of the colour of the shirt or suit.

The favourite knot at present is the Half Windsor, which
sits best under the cut-away collar.

Belts
Basic black leather – plus tan, oxblood or dark brown if you
have the shoes – is all that you really need.

Braces
Better kept invisible.

Shoes
Buy the best you can afford. Although you don't need
masses, you really must not wear the same pair two days
running. Shoes should always be clean, well fitting,
comfortable and not scuffed.

Generally, you need three types of black shoes:

1 Well structured like an Oxford Brogue or Derby *for
   suits and more formal jacket/trouser combinations*
2 A casual lace-up or slip-on *for smart/casual*

3 A soft shoe like a moccasin, Dockers, Doc Martens *for very casual*

Tan or oxblood can be worn selectively with other outfits – such as a navy jacket and grey trousers – but should always be complemented by a matching belt.

Briefcase
Only leather and not too shabby. Do not carry holdalls, sports bags etc. as a work bag.

Jewellery
Cufflinks etc, should reflect your personality and the occasion. A watch should also be sensible, manly and elegant, not funny or coloured plastic.

For women

Jewellery, scarves and belts can add interest when the overall effect is too one-dimensional. But do not wear accessories just for the sake of wearing them.

Jewellery
These should be subtle touches to customise and feminise your clothes. Gold, silver, pearl, bronze and pewter are always right. Not so small to be neither unnoticeable nor too big to overwhelm. A small chain or similar around the neck or a brooch finishes a simple well-cut suit.

Shoes
Buy the best you can afford and remember that you don't need masses. Basic core colours to build your wardrobe that works i.e. black, dark brown or navy – taupe or tan in warmer weather. Have different styles and heels for

different purposes but you can never go wrong with simple stylish Courts that are not too clumpy – or too 'mumsy'. Always protect with Scotchguard and re-apply regularly. Shoes should always be clean, well fitting, comfortable and not scuffed.

Bags
Go for the best you can afford and restrict yourself to basic items in standard colours. One does not need a whole wardrobe of handbags today – often a large squashy bag and small evening bag can suffice. It is best if you can to confine yourself to carrying one bag; choose a leather feminine soft briefcase that will also accommodate all your personal clutter in a small inner bag.

Hosiery
Sheer looking hosiery is fashionable but *Vaguely* or *Nearly Black* looks fine worn with most dark colours. Thick textured or opaque tights are rather passé now and should be restricted to very short or long skirts and chunky shoes, not worn with business suits.

Lingerie

Be measured regularly (one changes every few years) and expertly to ensure you are buying the right size; it can make the world of difference to both comfort and appearance. Panty girdles and control tights are definitely preferable to visible bulges.

The finishing touch – clever co-ordinating

- Clever co-ordinating is keeping co-ordinating simple. When creating an outfit, always work out which accessories you will add to complete it.
- Clever co-ordinating takes into account fabric and texture compatibility as well as colour.
- When combining separates of different colours, one item should contain some of the colour of the other by pattern, texture or trim. If it doesn't, you can create the link with your shoes (and belt).
- Clever co-ordinating depends on balance – the right length and width of garments must be judged: by your bodyshape, your proportion, and the combination of the garments themselves.

For women

- Keep to the basic colours – black, brown and navy. Remember that you don't need to wear brown clothes in order to have, and enjoy the benefit of, brown accessories, If you have the range of colours, choose which colour you will accessorise each outfit with by identifying:

- The most appropriate style for the circumstances.
- The most flattering complement.
- When combining separates of different colours you can create the link with accessories by adding a scarf or obvious jewellery in the other colour, in a pattern of both colours or in your basic accessory colour e.g. jet or tortoiseshell/amber.
- In order to complete a total picture that works, your clothes must be linked to your accessories.

CO-ORDINATING MADE EASY

Bottom layer	Col-our	Top layer	Colour	Middle layer colour
Dress	anyc	Jacket	Same as dress but diff compatible texture	n/a
	anyc		Pac & dress colour	n/a
	anyc		Ac	
Suit skirt	anyc	Suit jacket	Skirt colour	Same colour in a different texture
	anyc		Skirt colour	Light*
	anyc		Skirt colour	Pattern: suit + ac
	anyc		Same as skirt colour	Pattern: suit colour +
	anyc			small amt of light*
Skirt	ac	Jacket	ac in diff compatible texture	cc
	ac		ac in diff compatible texture	Ac + small amt of light*
	ac		ac in diff compatible texture	Light*
	ac		Suitable contrasting colour	ac
	ac		Suitable contrasting colour	Light*
	ac		Suitable contrasting colour	Pattern: top/ bottom colours

	ac	Suitable contrasting colour	Pattern: top/ bottom colours + min amt of light*
	ac	pac	Any suitable colour in the jacket
	ac	pac	Light*
	ac	pac	Pattern: pac and compatible to that of the jacket
Skirt	pac	ac	One of the skirt colours
	pac	ac	Light*
	cc	ac	Same as skirt
	cc	ac	Light*
	cc	ac	Pattern: top/ bottom colours
	cc	ac	Pattern: top/ bottom colours + small amt of light*
	cc	ac	Pattern: One of the colours + small amt of light*
Skirt	anyc	Any complimenting colour	ac
KEY:	Anyc = any colour	pac = pattern which includes ac	
	Ac = accessory colour	cc = contrasting colour	

*Light is whatever suits you and the clothes' colour best – white, cream, buttermilk, milk, ivory etc.

Acc = Accessory colour: black, brown or navy.

- You can usually do the same for cardigans as with jackets, depending on style.
- You can usually do the same for trousers as for skirts, depending on shape.
- If accessory is black, you can usually apply the same co-ordinating with grey.

The finishing touch – flattering fit

Do not be afraid to alter your clothes to you but do ensure it is done professionally. However, if a great deal needs to be changed, it would be best to find an alternative better-fitting garment.

- The two lapels and both shoulders should line up.
- Trousers will only be comfortable if the rise coincides with yours.#
- Neither jackets nor trousers can ever hang as they should with overloaded pockets.
- There should not be any gape on buttons or pull on trouser pleats or seams which indicates tightness.
- There should not be extra material between the shoulder and the waist, usually visible in a crease at the neck.#
- The sleeves (or trouser legs) should not be cut too wide for your frame generally.
- The back of the neck should sit tightly to the nape of your neck.
- The armhole should not be too deep.#
- Your shoulders should be compatible with the shoulder seam.
- Sit down and move your arms around to ensure comfort.

(#Usually alterations cannot alleviate this satisfactorily)

For men

- Length of jacket must not be shorter than the middle knuckle on the thumb – and usually the length of the fully extended thumb when hands are hanging straight.
- Trouser hemlines should just reach the shoe and then break by folding slightly inwards. They should be long enough to conceal the first few laces of a laced-up shoe and be about one and a half inches longer at the back than the front.

For women

- Bust should not be flattened.#
- The skirt should not be too wide at its base.
- Jackets should not finish just at your widest part – unless it's not too wide!
- Pockets and detail in the wrong place (e.g. bustline) draw attention to an area; they can often be moved or removed altogether.

Once you have considered all the outfits in the wardrobe in the light of the right co-ordinating and accessorising, all that is left to do is to go shopping. Intelligent shopping will make the most of your time, energy and budget whilst eliminating mistakes and impulse buys.

Intelligent shopping

Do's

- Use a back mirror to see your back view without turning.
- Wear socks/tights and shoes in the right colour.
- Wear a top or bottom that will complement what you're selecting.
- Only focus on one need at a time.
- Select to flatter your age, personality and shape.
- Check for good fit and proportion.
- From time to time review your self – nothing stays the same, especially us!
- Wear jewellery to dress up the potential purchase.*
- Wear make-up and ensure that your hair looks presentable.*

Dont's

- Don't stand on top of mirror but at least 2 ft away.
- Don't ask others for advice unless you respect their appearance.
- Buy all one label, just for convenience.
- *MUST HAVES:*
  'Seen it on someone/in a mag/shop window'
  'It's such a beautiful colour/fabric/pattern'
  'It's such a bargain'
  'Because a mag or TV programme said so'
  When I'm: 'thinner/tanned/have longer hair etc.'
- Panic buy for a special occasion.

- Be a fashion victim or a frump.
- Play safe with duplicates of what you already have – or go to the other extreme.
- Buy just because you don't want to go home without something.

This is almost the end of the week and you should be feeling very much more confident. You have examined both your presentation and your appearance. You now know what makes a positive business image and have applied it to yourself. All that we need to do now is make sure that your good work is maintained. It also must be reviewed from time to time as nothing stays exactly the same for long.

Summary

Now you should be well on your way to *your* wardrobe that works.

You have:
- weeded the current wardobe
- dealt with those clothes that need – and are worth – attention
- planned what you *need* to buy – and what you *would like* to buy
- learned how to put it all together:
    - to maximise the combinations;
    - to change the appearance;
    - to alter the functionality; and
    - to always look stylish.

Accessory and wardrobe maintenance

We have worked through the week on all aspects of your business image.

Now that the week is drawing to a close, it would be sensible to review what we have done and where you go from here.

What you now know about your image:

- the ways that you can use it
- the components that make it
- the importance of monitoring other people's assessment of it
- how to maximise all the ingredients to provide a congruent and positive image.

What now you must accept is that nothing stays exactly the same. There is still some work to do ... and probably always will be.

- Whenever there is any change in your life – a new job, location, promotion, a change in the season, etc. you need to re-appraise. Obviously, this mainly applies to your clothes but the other components must also be considered. For example, new situations may demand knowledge about different etiquette or manners.
- Taking into account that you have moved on during this last week, make sure that every three months you set aside a few hours to review your self again.

Armed with more confidence, you may well even take a few further steps.

- Now that you have a wardrobe that really works for *you*, you also have to work for *it* to ensure that it stays up to scratch.

Caring for your clothes

(* applies to women only)

- Leave clothes to air in room overnight; check for threads, stains etc. then only put away *when* they have been dealt with.
- Elastic waists should be hung on peg hangers to prevent stretched elastic.
- Knitwear is best on padded or non-slip hangers to avoid stretching.
- Cover little-worn items with plastic shoulder covers to keep dust-free.
- Always do up at least top button to keep shape and pull out sleeves.
- Pad out handbags with rags, old towels or tissue to keep shape.*
- Footwear. Always spray shoes with a protector before use *and re-apply regularly.* Check soles and heels regularly. Never wear the same shoes 2 days running. Always keep shoetrees in shoes. The best way is to invest in one pair of wooden trees and use them every night in the pair you take off. These absorb perspiration and make sure the shoes last longer keeping their shape. The next day, substitute

other trees and the wooden ones are then vacated for that day's pair again. Scuffed heels can be camouflaged with felt tip or a proprietary heel product.

- Suede should be regularly brushed with a special brush, using steam to remove stubborn stains. Faded suede can be well revitalised with DASCO spray in the appropriate colour.

- Patent is best cleaned with diluted washing-up liquid and dried well with a soft cloth.

- Faded or dingy under/nightwear can be saved and then dyed all together in tea or a snazzy colour.

- Don't pack away clothes in plastic, as some fabrics will discolour. Use old pillowcases or acid free paper.

- Always use a damp cloth when pressing clothes to avoid shine.

- Ties. After each wearing, untie the knot carefully. Leaving it knotted may cause permanent wrinkles. Always hang up your tie, in colours – use either a wooden tie rack, a rail or hanger. Never trap your tie under your car seat belt. This can cause silk to crease. Leave a few days in-between wearing a silk tie; hang the tie in a warm, moist environment to allow creases to drop out. Never wash or rub a silk tie and preserve by using a silk protector

Business trips can often put extra strain on the wardrobe. It is difficult to still look and feel your best living out of a suitcase without the facilities one has at home. The hints below may help you to maintain your image at home and abroad.

Packing your clothes

- Roll all knits – they will be fine.
- Cover suits totally etc. with dry cleaner type polythene covers to prevent creasing.
- Putting the clothes on hangers in the case saves masses of time on arrival.
- Put all small items like underwear and jewellery etc. in handbags and hats to keep their shape or in shoes.
- Always wrap cosmetics, toiletries and perfume in plastic or put in a separate bag.
- It's often easier to take a smaller suitcase and a separate holdall containing your shoes, bags, toiletries etc.
- Use the sides of a case for shoes, books, belts etc.
- Put the items that you are most likely to need on top, e.g. a clean shirt, in case of delays.

- Always wrap shoes if they may be dirty.
- If time is of the essence, hang complete outfits including accessories on one hanger, covered with polythene.
- If anything does crease, hang in the bathroom immediately and let the hot tap run with the door closed – the steam should do the trick. Hairdryers also work.

The wardrobe that works could quickly become the wardrobe that no longer works. It has to be, and stay, organised properly otherwise you could slip back into old habits.

Organising the wardrobe

Hanging

- To save wasting space, divide cupboard into full hanging and half hanging.
- If you have only full length hanging, you can create

2 levels by linking 2 hangers. Use 12 inches of chain around neck of first hanger and insert hook of new hanger through it.

- Only ever hang one garment on each hanger.
- Use uniform hangers for same type of garments e.g. trousers, jackets etc.
- Hang all items of one category together i.e. trousers, skirts etc.
- Scarves, ties, belts and necklaces can be hung on hooks on back of cupboard door.
- Cover little-worn items with plastic shoulder covers.
- Always do up at least top button to keep shape and pull out sleeves.
- Use bars of soap, empty perfume bottles or pomanders tied with ribbon to keep clothes smelling pleasant.
- Supermoths love natural fabrics. Ensure you use prevention; there is no cure.
- Hang shirts rather than fold them, even for packing, to minimise creasing.

Shoes
These should be graded by colour and use.

Underthings
These should be separated into plastic bags or containers –
drawer dividers are invaluable (from John Lewis).

Life has a way of playing nasty tricks – usually at the worst
time possible – so here are some survival hints.

Survival

- Keep needles threaded with light and black cotton in
  an easily accessed place.
- Keep all spare buttons, material cut off when
  shortening etc. in a little bag together. You never
  know when you might need them.
- Lead pencil releases sticky zips.
- Colourless nail varnish or hair spray will stop
  ladders running further.
- Use Selotape on dark clothes, particularly
  shoulders, to remove fluff or stray hairs.
- Shorten sleeves quickly by folding over and adding
  press-studs.
- Double-sided tape is invaluable for quick clothes
  patching and will hold 24 hours.
- Lingerie clips will hold your bra straps in place. Tape
  or pin scarves & throws to feel more secure – it
  won't show!
- Woolite for silk, wool, cotton and linen can often be
  used when labels say only dry cleaning and will be
  more effective with certain stains.

- Cashmere clinic at 020 7584 9806 for moth-nibbled garments.
- Invisible Mending: Neville Secchic at 01924 464281.
- Clothes and Accessory Dyeing advice: Dylon at 020 8663 4801.
- General advice: Good Housekeeping Institute at 020 7439 5000. Help number for clothes maintenance etc. is 09067 529090 which is open on Mondays, Wednesdays and Fridays beween 2:00pm and 4:30pm.

Stains

- Flush stains immediately with soda water.
- Blood   Soak in cold water with salt.
- Grease   Soak stain in washing-up liquid for 30 minutes then wash as normal.
- Pollen   Don't brush. Hold Selotape as near as you can without touching the fabric.
- Chocolate   Treat with glycerine and then rinse in warm soapy water.
- Lipstick   Dab with eucalyptus then rinse in warm soapy water.
- Perspiration   Dissolve Aspirin in warm water and soak.

Getting more from your work wardrobe than work – *for women*

- Clip earrings can dress up court shoes or a bag for evening.
- Worn under a jacket, a large scarf, or piece of

fabric, can substitute for a camisole or a blouse but secure it well.

- By adding a small piece of unobtrusive Velcro to a hat, it can then be re-trimmed to match different outfits by adding buttons, bows, feathers, braid etc.
- A small clutch bag can be converted temporarily into a shoulder bag (easier for drinks parties!) by the addition of a chain.
- Lighter weight blouses and jackets can be re-vamped by cutting off the sleeves; similarly trousers can become shorts.
- Trim a simple dress or 2 piece with diamante or jet braid or buttons for a quick DIY cocktail outfit.
- Create an outfit from a light coloured blouse and black skirt by changing blouse buttons to black (similarly with any other combination).

It is so easy to sit back and just carry on now that you have done so much good work. However, we need to prepare checks that can be carried out from time to time to ensure that the progress continues.

- Try the voice test with people who only meet you on the phone
- Deal with any mannerisms without becoming totally obsessed about them
- Look in a mirror to see how you are walking and moving.
- Are you: sitting neatly; smiling as much as you can … naturally; looking people straight in the eye when

talking to them; not looking worried, tense or nervous.

- Is your grooming up to scratch? Ensure that your skin always looks clean, even, blemish free and healthy. If you wear glasses, check every so often that they still look modern. Keep your teeth white. Change your daily aftershave or perfume sometimes. Make-up needs to be reviewed from time to time.
- The wardrobe most definitely needs to be reviewed each season and then dealt with accordingly. Requirements do change and you may not think of them in wardrobe terms until you start to do your wardrobe management all over again.

Summary

The week is over and you now have a managed image, which should certainly have helped you towards:

- Making a strong first impression
- Feeling good and looking good
- Getting more from people and situations
- Easing your way up the ladder of success
- Being viewed more positively by others

Be patient; Rome wasn't built in a day and it may take a little time to notice all the effects.

Good Luck!